MW01088107

CHRISTIANITY
STUDY
SERIES

A Closer Look at
Your Identity
in Christ

BOB
GEORGE

HARVEST HOUSE PUBLISHERS
Eugene, Oregon 97402

Cover by Terry Dugan Design, Minneapolis, Minnesota

A CLOSER LOOK AT YOUR IDENTITY IN CHRIST

Copyright © 1993 Harvest House Publishers
Eugene, Oregon 97402

ISBN 1-56507-084-4

Printed in the United States of America.

97 98 99 00 01 02 03 / CH / 13 12 11 10 9 8 7 6 5 4

Contents

No Other Foundation

As a person's physical growth is based on proper diet and exercise, so is the Christian's spiritual growth dependent on regular feeding upon the Word of God and application of its truth. With more false teaching, shifting opinions, and general confusion in the world than ever before, Christians need a solid foundation upon which to base their beliefs and build their lives. The Word of God declares that Jesus Christ is that foundation of truth. Therefore, the emphasis of the Classic Christianity Study Series is in helping Christians discover for themselves what the Bible actually says about Christ.

These Bible study guides are uniquely prepared for this purpose. They are useful for the newborn, intermediate, or mature Christian in that they begin with the fundamental and central question of who is Jesus Christ and then build upon that foundation in a logical and progressive manner. The Classic Christianity Study Series is also extremely flexible in that it can be used for individual or group study.

The Book of Acts tells us that the first Christians were "continually devoting themselves to the apostles' *teaching* and to *fellowship*, to the *breaking of bread* and to *prayer*" (Acts 2:42 NASB). The need for a proper balance in the Christian life is as real today as it was in the first century. The Classic Christianity Study Series has therefore been designed to incorporate all of these elements vital for spiritual growth.

> *For no man can lay a foundation other than the one which is laid, which is Jesus Christ* (1 Corinthians 3:11 NASB).

Helpful Suggestions
as You Begin

1. Choosing a convenient time and location will help you to be consistent in your study.

2. Use a Bible that you are comfortable with.

3. Before beginning your study, always pray and ask God to quiet your heart and open your mind to understand the Scriptures.

4. Approach the Word of God with a learner's heart and a teachable spirit.

1

In Search of an Identity

The issue of identity is inescapable and central to our lives. "Who am I?" we all ask. "Where did I come from? Where am I going?" Every person wrestles with these questions, and the answers we adopt determine the direction of our lives.

Today, this search for identity falls under the concept of *self-image*. Every person has some image of himself. It could be a healthy, positive image, or it could be a poor, negative one. Regardless, a person's self-image determines his self-worth in this life, whether he is a success or a failure. Self-image is what affects, for better or worse, a person's attitude and behavior toward others and life's circumstances. With all that is at stake, it is easy to see why people are in search of a good self-image.

However, there is much debate concerning how to develop a good self-image. Many psychologists, counselors, and even some church leaders believe that to develop a good self-image a person needs to start loving himself more. As we will see, this philosophy is contrary to the teaching of the Word of God. Paul writes in 2 Timothy 3:2 that in the last days men will be lovers of themselves. According to this verse, our problem is that we love ourselves *too* much. So it would appear we could not develop a good self-image based on learning to love ourselves more. As a matter of fact, we do not need to develop a *good* self-image at all. What we need to develop is a realistic view of ourselves, what I like to call a *proper self-image*. We need to learn who we are from God's perspective.

Key Verse: Romans 12:3

For by the grace given me I say to every one of you: Do not think of yourself more highly than you ought, but rather think of yourself with sober judgment, in accordance with the measure of faith God has given you.

---

1. What is Paul's warning to us regarding how we should think about ourselves?

2. What motivated Paul to say we shouldn't think more highly of ourselves than we ought?

3. In your opinion, what would motivate a person to think more highly of himself than he ought?

4. Pride is what caused Satan to be cast from heaven. Pride is what caused Adam to eat of the tree of the knowledge of good and evil. And pride is what motivates us to think of ourselves more highly than we ought. How does Paul tell us to think about ourselves to counteract this attitude of pride?

5. When we think of ourselves with sober judgment, what are we thinking in accordance to?

6. How does this verse compare to the modern-day philosophy that says we need to love ourselves more?

But mark this: There will be terrible times in the last days. People will be lovers of themselves, lovers of money, boastful, proud, abusive,

disobedient to their parents, ungrateful, unholy, without love, un-
forgiving, slanderous, without self-control, brutal, not lovers of the
good, treacherous, rash, conceited, lovers of pleasure rather than lovers
of God—having a form of godliness but denying its power (2 Timothy
3:1-5).

1. What characteristic of people during the last days does Paul list first?

2. Is the problem of man that we hate ourselves or that we love ourselves too much?

3. In light of these verses, will loving ourselves more enable us to develop a proper self-image?

How to Develop a Proper Self-Image

To develop a proper self-image, we must first decide who we are going to listen to: Satan and the world, or God and His Word. We have already seen that Satan and the world are in direct opposition to God and His Word concerning how we should think about ourselves. Unfortunately, we live in the world and are constantly bombarded by the philosophies of the world. So let's examine some of the ways to determine self-image from the world's perspective and then counter them with what God has to say.

Appearance

1. How we look is certainly one way we determine our self-image. What will your self-image be if you think you are pretty or handsome?

2. What will it be if you think you are ugly?

3. If you truly are pretty or handsome, what will happen to your self-image as you grow older and your looks change, or if you are in an accident that alters your appearance?

4. Who helps you determine if you are pretty or handsome?

5. Usually Mom and Dad start by saying, "You are a beautiful little girl," or "You are a fine-looking young boy." Friends and complete strangers can echo these same sentiments. From these opinions it is easy to develop a positive self-image. But can the opinions of Mom and Dad, friends, and strangers change?

6. One day, you may have decided yourself you are good-looking. Does your opinion of your appearance ever change?

7. Can you ever develop a secure self-image or identity based on your appearance?

> *For you created my inmost being; you knit me together in my mother's womb. I praise you because I am fearfully and wonderfully made; your works are wonderful, I know that full well* (Psalm 139:13,14).

1. According to these verses, who made you the way you are?

2. Since God made you the way you are, does it make sense to build a self-image based on what others say about you, or even what you say about yourself?

Abilities

We also determine our identity by what we do: I'm a businessman, a housewife, or a football player, for example. Self-image based on what we do, however, is dependent on how well we perform.

1. What would your self-image be if as a businessman, your business failed? Or if a mother, your kids turned out to be drug addicts?

2. Do your abilities to perform a function change with time? For example, is a 45-year-old athlete able to perform the way he did at the age of 25?

3. Who determines whether you are good or bad at something?

4. Would their opinions ever change?

5. Are there other people out there who have greater abilities than you?

6. In comparison to them, what would your self-image be?

> *We do not dare to classify or compare ourselves with some who commend themselves. When they measure themselves by themselves and compare themselves with themselves, they are not wise* (2 Corinthians 10:12).

1. According to this verse, is it wise to compare yourself to others?

2. What two conclusions could you come to if you compared yourself to others?

3. You could conclude that you are better than someone else and that leads to pride. Or you could conclude that you are worse than someone else and that leads to self-condemnation. Are either of these attitudes from God?

4. Does it make sense to build your self-image on your abilities as a person?

There are many other ways we try to determine our self-image based on the philosophies of the world (for example, family relationships, friends, denominational affiliation). Basically, however, all these standards determine self-image by one of three things: (1) what others think about you; (2) what you think others think about you; and (3) what you think about yourself. And this brings us to the problem in listening to the world's opinions in regard to who we are. The world's opinions are constantly changing from moment to moment. It is impossible to find any stability or security in what the world says concerning our identity.

1. What will a person experience if he has a poor self-image based on the opinions of the world?

> *For everything in the world—the cravings of sinful man, the lust of his eyes and the boasting of what he has and does—comes not from the Father but from the world. The world and its desires pass away, but the man who does the will of God lives forever* (1 John 2:16,17).

2. What does this verse say is in the world?

3. Do the cravings of sinful man, the lust of his eyes, and the boasting of what he has and does come from the Father?

4. Where do these things come from?

5. If a person is dependent on what is in the world to determine his identity, according to this verse what is this person dependent on?

6. What happens to the world and its desires?

7. Since the things of the world pass away, can a person ever have a secure identity if he is dependent on the things of this world to determine who he is?

8. Based on this verse, why do you think it is important to see yourself from God's perspective rather than the world's?

We do not need a self-image based on the ever-changing opinions of the world. We need a proper self-image, an identity based on truth from God's perspective. Since God created us and knows us better than we know ourselves, it makes sense to begin listening to what He says about us.

You are not who you are because of your own or others' opinions. You are who you are because of what God says about you. When we begin listening to God, we can rest assured that what He says will not be like the ever-changing opinions of the world: "All men are like grass, and all their glory is like the flowers of the field; the grass withers and the flowers fall, but the word of the Lord stands forever" (1 Peter 1:24,25).

In the next chapter, we will take a closer look at what God says about you and me.

2

A New
Identity

A person has no identity apart from a relationship with someone or something else. That is why we latch onto practically anything in our desperate need to discover who we are. We determine our identity through our appearance, occupation, abilities, family relationships, friends, denominational affiliation—the list is endless.

Identity, however, is a spiritual need. Who we truly are is determined by our relationship to Jesus Christ. When we are identified with Him, we have an identity that cannot be shaken or taken away. It's an identity that is more wonderful than we could ever imagine.

Unfortunately, the tragedy of modern-day Christianity is our utter ignorance of who we are in Christ. As a result, many Christians struggle, wondering if God loves them. The believer's identity in Christ is not a side issue; it is central to experiencing the real Christian life.

Key Verse: 1 Corinthians 15:22

For as in Adam all die, so in Christ all will be made alive.

1. From God's point of view, there are only two kinds of people in this world.

Their identities are determined by who they are identified with. What two people does the verse say we can be identified with?

2. What phrase does Paul use to show that people are either identified with Adam or identified with Christ?

3. To be "in Adam" or "in Christ" is strange language to us. Biblically, to be "in" someone means that person is our family head. As such, he has left us his name, his nature, an inheritance, and a destiny. What is the destiny for those who are "in Adam"?

4. What is the destiny for those who are "in Christ"?

Every human being is born into this world "in Adam." That means we are born with the same nature, inheritance, and destiny that Adam possessed after his fall. Let's take a closer look at the inheritance left to us by Adam.

> *For just as through the disobedience of the one man the many were made sinners . . .* (Romans 5:19).

1. What were we made through the disobedience of the one man?

2. Who was this one man?

3. Therefore, what is our identity in Adam?

> *Therefore, just as sin entered the world through one man, and death through sin, and in this way death came to all men, because all sinned* (Romans 5:12).

1. How did sin enter the world?

2. Who was this one man?

3. What entered the world through sin?

4. As a result, what came to all men?

5. Why?

6. Therefore, what did Adam pass on to you and me?

> *As for you, you were dead in your transgressions and sins, in which you used to live when you followed the ways of this world and of the ruler of the kingdom of the air, the spirit who is now at work in those who are disobedient. All of us also lived among them at one time, gratifying the cravings of our sinful nature and following its desires and thoughts. Like the rest, we were by nature objects of wrath* (Ephesians 2:1-3).

1. According to this passage, what were we in our transgressions and sins?

2. What ways did we follow when we lived in our transgressions and sins?

3. When we were dead in our sins, what did we seek to gratify?

4. What desires and thoughts did we follow?

5. When we were dead in our sins, what were we by nature?

6. What type of nature and lifestyle did Adam pass on to us as our family head?

7. What destiny did Adam hand down to us?

All of us are born into this world as sinners. We each were born dead in our sins and totally controlled by our sinful nature. As a result, we were by nature objects of wrath. This is the identity Adam passed on to us—an identity we received through birth. For this identity to change requires a new birth.

> *In reply Jesus declared, "I tell you the truth, no one can see the kingdom of God unless he is born again." . . . Jesus answered, " I tell you the truth, no one can enter the kingdom of God unless he is born of water and the Spirit. Flesh gives birth to flesh, but the Spirit gives birth to spirit"* (John 3:3,5,6).

1. What did Jesus say must happen to a person for that person to see the kingdom of God?

2. What did Jesus say must happen to a person for that person to enter the kingdom of God?

3. John describes being born of water as "flesh gives birth to flesh." This is a picture of our physical birth. What kind of birth is Jesus referring to when He says, "You must be born again"?

4. Physically, we are born "in Adam" and he is our family head. When we are born again of the Spirit of God, who becomes our family head?

5. Therefore, who does a person's identity come from once he has been born again?

When Nicodemus heard Jesus say you must be born again, Nicodemus asked, "How can this be?" This is a very natural question. How *can* you be born again? Jesus gives the answer in John 3:16.

> For God so loved the world that he gave his one and only Son, that whoever believes in him shall not perish but have eternal life (John 3:16).

1. What motivated God to give His one and only Son?

2. Why did God give us His Son?

3. What does this verse say we must do to inherit eternal life?

4. Then, how are we born again?

> Yet to all who received him, to those who believed in his name, he gave the right to become children of God—children born not of natural descent, nor of human decision or a husband's will, but born of God (John 1:12,13).

1. What happens to those who receive Jesus Christ?

2. How does John say we receive Jesus Christ?

3. A child of God is born of whom?

4. Why do you think John shows the contrast between being born of natural descent and being born of God?

5. If you believe in Jesus Christ and are born again, what is your new identity?

> *For you did not receive a spirit that makes you a slave again to fear, but you received the Spirit of sonship. And by him we cry, "Abba, Father." The Spirit himself testifies with our spirit that we are God's children. Now if we are children, then we are heirs—heirs of God and co-heirs with Christ, if indeed we share in his sufferings in order that we may also share in his glory* (Romans 8:15-17).

1. When you were born again of the Spirit of God, what Spirit does Paul say you received?

2. What kind of spirit does Paul contrast the Spirit of sonship to?

3. In Ephesians 2:3, we learned that "in Adam" we were all by nature objects of wrath and our natural response to God is one of fear. In light of this, how important is it to understand that when we are born again, we do not receive a spirit that makes us a slave to fear?

4. Because we have received the Spirit of sonship, what do we cry out to God?

5. What does the Spirit of God testify to our human spirits?

6. Because we are children of God, what else have we become?

7. Therefore, who does our inheritance come from now?

A person's identity is determined by who he is identified with. From God's vantage point, a person is either identified with Adam or with Jesus Christ. If you are identified with Adam, you are a sinner and your destiny is eternal separation from God—death. If you are identified with Jesus Christ, you are a child of God and your destiny is eternal life.

Your identity can change through a new birth. If you are "in Adam," are you willing to receive Jesus Christ by believing in His name and experiencing new birth in Christ? You can do so by simply asking Jesus to come into your heart. The following is a suggested prayer:

> *Lord Jesus, I need You. I recognize that I was born into this world a sinner, dead and in need of life. Thank You for dying for the forgiveness of my sins and then for being raised from the dead so You could come and give me life. I now receive You into my heart. Take control of my life and teach me about Your love and the inheritance I now have as a child of God. Thank You for coming into my heart and for giving me eternal life.*

If you prayed to receive Christ, you are now a child of God. You have a new identity, a new nature, and a new destiny. Throughout the rest of the book, we will take a closer look at just what it means to be a child of God and the marvelous inheritance we have as His children.

3

You Are a Brand New Creation

When you become a child of God, the Bible says you have become a brand new creation—like a caterpillar becomes a beautiful butterfly. In nature, the caterpillar weaves a cocoon around itself, and in the cocoon the marvelous process of metamorphosis takes place. When this process is complete, a beautiful butterfly emerges. This butterfly is a new creature; it will never be a caterpillar again. In the same way, we have become new creatures in Christ; we will never be old sinners again. And as new creatures in Christ, we must learn to see ourselves as God sees us.

Key Verse: 2 Corinthians 5:17

Therefore, if anyone is in Christ, he is a new creation; the old has gone, the new has come!

1. If you are in Christ, what have you become?

2. According to this verse, what has happened to the old?

3. Once we have become a new creation in Christ, can we ever become a lost person again?

4. What does this verse say has come?

You would never look at a butterfly and say, "Look at that good-looking converted caterpillar." Why? Because now it is a new creature and you don't think of a butterfly in terms of what it once was. I constantly hear Christians, however, referring to themselves as "old sinners saved by grace." Even though we were sinners, that is not our identity today.

> *Paul, an apostle of Christ Jesus by the will of God, to the saints in Ephesus, the faithful in Christ Jesus* (Ephesians 1:1).

1. In his letter to the Ephesians, how did Paul address the believers there?

2. Did Paul think of the believers in Ephesus as "old sinners saved by grace"?

3. According to this verse, what is our identity?

4. Does God see us as "old sinners saved by grace" or as "saints"?

5. How do you see yourself?

> *Paul, an apostle of Christ Jesus by the will of God, and Timothy our brother, to the church of God in Corinth, together with all the saints throughout Achaia* (2 Corinthians 1:1).

1. Corinth was a city in the Roman province of Achaia. How did Paul address the believers in Corinth?

2. Members of the Corinthian church were guilty of sexual sins, getting drunk at the Lord's supper, and pride. Yet with all this going on, God, through Paul, calls the Corinthian believers *saints*. In light of this, what can you conclude about the role behavior plays in determining a believer's identity from God's vantage point?

3. Is it possible for you as a child of God, a saint, to commit sins?

4. Does the fact that you commit sins determine your identity in Christ?

5. What makes you a saint in God's eyes?

6. When you sin as a child of God, who is it that is doing the sinning?

7. How does God see you when you sin?

8. How do you see yourself?

9. Is there a difference between how God sees you and how you see yourself?

10. If so, are you willing to see yourself as a saint?

As Christians we sometimes get the idea that our behavior is what is truly important to God, that all He is concerned with is what we do. Behavior, however, is simply the result of a belief system. There is an old adage that says, "Actions follow attitude." That is why God is so persistent in teaching us *who* we are. Once we know and truly believe we are children of God, saints by calling, our actions will follow suit. As we will see in the following verses, knowing who we are is our true motivation for living godly lives.

> *As a prisoner for the Lord, then, I urge you to live a life worthy of the calling you have received* (Ephesians 4:1).

1. According to this verse, what kind of life does Paul urge us to live?

2. If you do not know or understand the calling you have received, can you live a life worthy of that calling?

> *To all in Rome who are loved by God and called to be saints: Grace and peace to you from God our Father and from the Lord Jesus Christ* (Romans 1:7).

1. According to this verse, what are we called to be?

2. So, what kind of life are we to live?

> *For you were once darkness, but now you are light in the Lord. Live as children of light* (Ephesians 5:8).

1. What does this verse say we once were?

2. In the Lord, what are we?

3. How, then, should we live?

4. Why should we live as children of light?

A good paraphrase of this verse is, "You once were a caterpillar, but now you are a butterfly. Fly like a butterfly!" It just makes sense for a butterfly to fly. In the same way, as children of God, saints by calling, it just makes sense for us to live in accordance with who we are. When we do sin, however, God doesn't try to correct our behavior. He reasons with us based on our identity.

It's as if He holds a mirror over us and says, "Look up here. What do you see?"

"A butterfly, Lord."

"Since you are a butterfly, why are you crawling around with the caterpillars?"

"I don't know, Lord. It doesn't make sense, does it?"

"No it doesn't. Why don't you get up and fly like a butterfly?"

The butterfly can fly because through the process of metamorphosis, God equipped the butterfly with wings. It wouldn't make any sense to tell the butterfly to fly if it didn't have wings. In the same way, it would be foolish to tell us to live a life worthy of our calling if we had not been given the Holy Spirit to enable us to do so. We have been made into a new creation, but what is it that makes us new?

> *To them God has chosen to make known among the Gentiles the glorious riches of this mystery, which is Christ in you, the hope of glory* (Colossians 1:27).

1. What is the mystery that Paul has made known to the Gentiles?

2. According to this verse, what makes us new creatures?

3. Who is our hope for living out and experiencing our calling as children of God?

4. Just as the butterfly is dependent on its wings to enable it to fly, who are we to be dependent on to live the Christian life?

> *I have been crucified with Christ and I no longer live, but Christ lives in me. The life I live in the body, I live by faith in the Son of God, who loved me and gave himself for me* (Galatians 2:20).

1. For what reason can Paul say, "I no longer live"?

2. Who does live in us?

3. Once again, what makes us new creatures in Christ?

4. According to this verse, how are we to live our lives?

You truly are a new creature in Christ. Through spiritual birth God has transformed you into a saint. You may act like an old sinner saved by grace, but that is not your identity. If you have been crawling around with the caterpillars, you need to realize that you are a butterfly. Get up and fly! God has something better for you than crawling around with the caterpillars. It is called the abundant life. With Christ living in you, you can experience everything God created you to be as a new creature in Christ.

4

You Are
Totally Forgiven

Having a proper understanding of our identity in Christ greatly depends on how we view God's forgiveness toward us. If we see ourselves as unforgiven or not worthy of forgiveness, it perverts our understanding of God's love. In a world where forgiveness has to be earned or paid for, complete and unconditional forgiveness is sometimes difficult to understand. However, the Scriptures tell us that this is the way God has forgiven us.

When Christ died on the cross, His last words were, "It is finished." In other words, "The payment for sin has been satisfied." All of the world's sins—past, present, and future—were paid for. This is the freedom we have as children of God. As 2 Corinthians 5:19 says, God is no longer "counting men's sins against them."

Key Verse: Acts 10:43

All the prophets testify about him that everyone who believes in him receives forgiveness of sins through his name.

---

1. Who do the prophets testify about?

2. What must one do to receive forgiveness of sins?

3. In light of this verse, what were the prophets in the Old Testament expecting the Messiah to do? Did He fulfill His mission?

4. When you put your faith in Christ, what did you receive?

5. According to this verse, what is part of your identity in Christ?

> *I will rescue you from your own people and from the Gentiles. I am sending you to them to open their eyes and turn them from darkness to light, and from the power of Satan to God, so that they may receive forgiveness of sins and a place among those who are sanctified by faith in me* (Acts 26:17,18).

1. According to these verses, what was Paul's mission?

2. Who were we under the power of before coming to Christ?

3. What do we receive upon putting our faith in Christ?

4. How are we sanctified?

5. If we are forgiven and sanctified when we put our faith in Christ, is there a need to be sanctified and forgiven at any subsequent time after our salvation?

6. When we become a child of God, what do we receive as part of our inheritance?

> *For he has rescued us from the dominion of darkness and brought us into the kingdom of the Son he loves, in whom we have redemption, the forgiveness of sins* (Colossians 1:13,14).

1. What has God rescued us from?

2. What do we have in Christ?

3. At what point were we redeemed?

4. At what point were we forgiven?

5. Does this verse say that forgiveness and redemption is a present-day reality or something we must ask for on a daily basis?

6. In light of all the previous verses, it is quite clear that our forgiveness was complete on the day we put our faith in Christ. Are you willing to rest in the fact that you are totally forgiven and that there is nothing you can do to add to it?

> *Then he adds: "Their sins and lawless acts I will remember no more." And where these have been forgiven, there is no longer any sacrifice for sin* (Hebrews 10:17,18).

1. What is it that God won't remember?

2. Why won't He remember them?

3. If God has forgiven our sins and remembers them no more, how, then, should we look at our sins?

4. How does this understanding make you feel about your relationship with God?

5. Is there anything to be fearful of in our relationship with God?

> *There is no fear in love. But perfect love drives out fear, because fear has to do with punishment. The one who fears is not made perfect in love. We love because he first loved us* (1 John 4:18,19).

1. According to this verse, if someone is fearful, what is he fearful of?

2. What would make us fearful of God's punishment?

3. What is it that drives out fear?

4. In the same way, what is it that drives out love?

5. Can we be fearful and loving at the same time?

6. How can we love God?

7. How does knowing that you are forgiven take away the fear of God's punishment?

> *Therefore, brothers, since we have confidence to enter the Most Holy Place by the blood of Jesus, by a new and living way opened for us*

through the curtain, that is, his body, and since we have a great priest over the house of God, let us draw near to God with a sincere heart in full assurance of faith, having our hearts sprinkled to cleanse us from a guilty conscience and having our bodies washed with pure water. Let us hold unswervingly to the hope we profess, for he who promised is faithful (Hebrews 10:19-23).

1. How did Jesus open the way for us to the Most Holy Place?

2. What is the Most Holy Place?

3. Who is our great priest?

4. Does knowing that you are forgiven give you confidence to approach God?

5. What is it that cleanses us from a guilty conscience?

6. With what attitude are we to draw near to God?

7. According to verse 23, who is it that is faithful, us or Him?

8. Why do you think it is important to know that part of your inheritance as a child of God is total forgiveness?

In him and through faith in him we may approach God with freedom and confidence (Ephesians 3:12).

1. In light of this verse, how may we approach God?

2. What does it mean to approach God with freedom and confidence?

3. How can we have freedom?

4. We have seen that our relationship with God should be greatly affected by the forgiveness Christ has provided. Is there any reason why you are not experiencing the freedom and confidence in your relationship with God? If so, are you willing to let go of it and by faith accept the fact that as a child of God you are totally forgiven and that this is your identity?

Our understanding of God's forgiveness has a lot to do with how we treat other people. If we have never experienced God's love and forgiveness for ourselves, it is very hard to be loving and forgiving toward others.

> *Be kind and compassionate to one another, forgiving each other, just as in Christ God forgave you* (Ephesians 4:32).

1. Why are we to forgive others?

2. How did God forgive us?

3. If God has forgiven us totally and unconditionally, how should we forgive others?

4. If we see ourselves as unforgiven or in danger of punishment, how will we treat others?

5. If we see ourselves as forgiven, how will we treat others?

> *Therefore, as God's chosen people, holy and dearly loved, clothe yourselves with compassion, kindness, humility, gentleness and patience.*

> *Bear with each other and forgive whatever grievances you may have against one another. Forgive as the Lord forgave you* (Colossians 3:12,13).

1. How are we described as God's people in this passage?

2. What are we to clothe ourselves with?

3. A forgiving spirit is totally natural for God's people. Why is this?

4. How many sins did Christ forgive us of?

5. How many grievances are we to forgive others of?

As we have seen, forgiveness is at the very root of our identity in Christ. His unconditional love for us that He demonstrated by dying on the cross is what gives us the power to draw near to God and to love others.

5

You Are
Totally Righteous

Not only did Jesus die to forgive us of our sin, but He also rose from the dead to live in us. When we receive Christ, we receive His righteousness because He is totally righteous. This life that we now share with Him is a totally righteous life. The righteousness of God that has been given through Jesus Christ is not dependent on our ability to stay holy. It is a completely free gift given to us when we put our faith in Christ. We have exchanged our unrighteousness for His perfect righteousness.

Understanding that we are as righteous as Jesus Christ because He lives in us is what frees us from the impossible task of trying to keep ourselves "clean" before God. Let's look at some Scriptures concerning the issue of righteousness.

Key Verse: Romans 3:21,22

But now a righteousness from God, apart from law, has been made known, to which the Law and the Prophets testify. This righteousness from God comes through faith in Jesus Christ to all who believe.

1. Where does true righteousness come from?

2. Can we become righteous by observing the law?

3. If not from the law, then how do we attain righteousness?

4. Who is it available to?

> *God made him who had no sin to be sin for us, so that in him we might become the righteousness of God* (2 Corinthians 5:21).

1. Did Christ have any sin?

2. What did God make Christ to be on our behalf?

3. How much of our sin do you think Christ took?

4. Because of this exchange, what did we become?

5. Where do we become the righteousness of God?

6. If we have become the righteousness of God, how righteous are we?

7. What is part of our inheritance in Christ as children of God?

> *However, to the man who does not work but trusts God who justifies the wicked, his faith is credited as righteousness* (Romans 4:5).

1. Who does God justify?

2. Is a man justified by his works or by trusting God?

3. To those who believe, what is credited to them?

4. If a person could gain righteousness by his own good works, whose righteousness would it be?

5. Whose righteousness is it when we believe God?

Just as through Adam we were all born spiritually dead, through Christ we are born spiritually alive. In Adam we are born in sin; in Christ we are born in righteousness. This is what it means to be "born again."

> *For if, by the trespass of the one man, death reigned through that one man, how much more will those who receive God's abundant provision of grace and of the gift of righteousness reign in life through the one man, Jesus Christ* (Romans 5:17).

1. What was the result of one man's sin?

2. How many people were affected by that one man's sin?

3. What is God's gift to those who will receive it?

4. What does it mean to "reign in life"?

> *What is more, I consider everything a loss compared to the surpassing greatness of knowing Christ Jesus my Lord, for whose sake I have lost all things. I consider them rubbish, that I may gain Christ and be found in him, not having a righteousness of my own that comes from the law, but that which is through faith in Christ—the righteousness that comes from God and is by faith* (Philippians 3:8,9).

1. What kind of righteousness does obedience to the law produce?

2. What kind of righteousness does faith in Christ produce?

3. Whose righteousness would you rather have, your own or God's?

4. There is only one way to receive the righteousness of God—by faith in Christ and His finished work at Calvary. Are you willing to give up on your feeble efforts and rest in His free gift of righteousness today?

5. If you are standing in the righteousness of Jesus Christ, how acceptable are you to God?

> *. . . to the praise of the glory of His grace, by which He made us accepted in the Beloved* (Ephesians 1:6 NKJV).

1. According to this verse, is our acceptance before God something we can establish?

2. Who has made us accepted?

3. If we are righteous and accepted by God, how, then, should we relate to Him?

It is important to understand that the righteousness of God is not just another gift He gives us. Righteousness is given in the form of a person, Jesus Christ the righteous one.

> *I am not ashamed of the gospel, because it is the power of God for the salvation of everyone who believes: first for the Jew, then for the Gentile. For in the gospel a righteousness from God is revealed, a righteousness that is by faith from first to last, just as it is written: "The righteous will live by faith"* (Romans 1:16,17).

1. What does Paul say he is not ashamed of?

2. What does the gospel reveal?

3. What is the power of the gospel?

4. How does someone receive the righteousness of God?

5. The righteousness of God is received by faith. How, then, do we continue to live?

6. Are you experiencing the power of the gospel in your life?

7. If not, are you willing to rest in the righteousness you have received as a child of God?

As we have seen, since we have been given the very righteousness of God, we can approach Him with great confidence, knowing that we don't stand in our own righteousness. There is nothing we can be condemned of if we are righteous. Our identity as children of God is based on His acceptance of us not because of our performance, but because of the righteous life of Christ that dwells in us.

6

You Are Reconciled

Reconciliation is an accounting term. Each month when you receive your bank statement you reconcile your account, making sure your balance equals the bank's balance. Through His death 2000 years ago, Christ balanced the books of justice. We owed a debt we could not pay; He paid a debt He did not owe. We are no longer in debt. Our penalty has been paid. We have been reconciled.

Knowing we have been reconciled to God by Christ's death changes our relationship to God. Once we were God's enemies, but now because of the death of His Son we are His friends.

Key Verse: Romans 5:10,11

For if, when we were God's enemies, we were reconciled to him through the death of his Son, how much more, having been reconciled, shall we be saved through his life! Not only is this so, but we also rejoice in God through our Lord Jesus Christ, through whom we have now received reconciliation.

1. According to these verses, how were we reconciled to God?

2. Does the verb tense indicate that being reconciled to God is something that will happen or something that has already happened?

3. Describe our relationship to God when we were reconciled.

4. What do you think it means to be God's enemy?

5. Having been reconciled, what can we be assured of?

6. If God reconciled the books of justice by reconciling us to Himself while we were His enemies, what kind of treatment can we expect from God now that we are His children?

7. According to this verse, what causes us to rejoice in God for our Lord Jesus Christ?

8. Could we rejoice if we had not received the reconciliation that God provided through the death of His Son?

9. Have you received the reconciliation that God provided through the death of His Son?

For God was pleased to have all his fullness dwell in him, and through him to reconcile to himself all things, whether things on earth or things in heaven, by making peace through his blood, shed on the cross. Once you were alienated from God and were enemies in your minds because of your evil behavior. But now he has reconciled you by

> *Christ's physical body through death to present you holy in his sight, without blemish and free from accusation* (Colossians 1:19-22).

1. How many things did God reconcile to Himself through Jesus Christ?

2. What was the result of Christ's shed blood on the cross for you and me?

3. When peace is established between enemies, it means they are no longer at war. Since Christ has made peace through His blood, are you at peace with Him? Or do you still consider yourself His enemy?

4. What do these verses say we once were in relationship to God?

5. These verses say we were enemies with God in our minds. Why did we think we were God's enemies?

6. Through Christ's death we have been reconciled. Because of this, how does God see us?

7. Because He sees us as holy in His sight, without blemish and accusation, what does this tell us about our evil behavior?

8. We may have thought we were God's enemies because of our evil behavior, but was God ever our enemy?

9. Could you consider someone who had reconciled you unto himself through the death of his son an enemy?

Greater love has no one than this, that he lay down his life for his friends (John 15:13).

1. What is the greatest love a person can have for another?

2. What did Christ do for you and me 2000 years ago?

3. What does this verse tell you about how God views us? Are we His friends or His enemies?

I no longer call you servants, because a servant does not know his master's business. Instead, I have called you friends, for everything that I learned from my Father I have made known to you (John 15:15).

1. Why does Jesus no longer call us servants?

2. What does He call us?

3. What has He made known to us?

All this is from God, who reconciled us to himself through Christ and gave us the ministry of reconciliation: that God was reconciling the world to himself in Christ, not counting men's sins against them. And he has committed to us the message of reconciliation. We are therefore Christ's ambassadors, as though God were making his appeal through us. We implore you on Christ's behalf: Be reconciled to God (2 Corinthians 5:18-20).

1. The reconciliation we have received through Christ came from whom?

2. What kind of ministry did God give us?

3. What is this ministry of reconciliation?

4. How does knowing that God no longer counts your sins against you change your relationship to God?

5. What message has He committed to us that we are to share to others?

6. Because we have been given this ministry of reconciliation, how does Paul describe us in our role here on this earth?

7. What appeal can we make to others on Christ's behalf?

8. What do you think the appeal "be reconciled to God" means?

> *Let us then approach the throne of grace with confidence, so that we may receive mercy and find grace to help us in our time of need* (Hebrews 4:16).

1. What does this verse tell us to do?

2. With what attitude are we to approach the throne of grace?

3. Could we approach the throne of grace with confidence if we still considered ourselves God's enemy?

4. If you still considered yourself an enemy of God, what would you expect to receive from Him if you approached Him?

5. What does this verse say we will receive in our time of need?

6. Can you see how important it is to understand that part of your identity in Christ is that you have been reconciled to God?

Reconciliation is a vital part of your identity in Christ. Through Christ's death 2000 years ago He reconciled you unto Himself. He demonstrated His love for you there. He showed that He never considered you His enemy, but that He laid down His life for you as His friend. When we receive this reconciliation we realize that God sees us as holy in His sight and free of accusations. There is no longer a sin barrier between you and God. It has been taken away.

Through this reconciliation you can approach the throne of grace with confidence, knowing that when you do you will receive grace and mercy in your time of need.

7

You Are Redeemed

Perhaps as a kid the last words you would hear from your parents before walking out the door for an evening of fun were, "Remember who you belong to." Your parents were hoping that the knowledge of who you were and who you belonged to would influence your decision-making process should you be tempted with the ways of the world.

Through our identity in Christ, God, too, reminds us "who we belong to." As children of God, we have been redeemed. To redeem means to buy back and then set free. We were born into this world in bondage to the law of sin and death. God purchased us out of this bondage through the death of His Son. That was the price the law demanded. Now we belong to God. He did not purchase us, however, to make us slaves again. He purchased us so we could receive the full rights as sons.

Key Verse: Colossians 1:13,14

For he has rescued us from the dominion of darkness and brought us into the kingdom of the Son he loves, in whom we have redemption, the forgiveness of sins.

1. According to this verse, what have we been rescued from?

2. Who rescued us from the dominion of darkness?

3. What kingdom have we been brought into?

4. In this kingdom of the Son He loves, what do we have?

5. According to this verse, is redemption and forgiveness something the believer presently possesses or something he must acquire?

6. If you are in Christ, a child of God, what is your inheritance and identity?

> *But when the time had fully come, God sent his Son, born of a woman, born under law, to redeem those under law, that we might receive the full rights of sons* (Galatians 4:4,5).

1. Why did God send His Son into the world?

2. For what purpose did Christ redeem us from the law?

3. Why do you think it is important to understand the significance of being redeemed?

> *When he came to his senses, he said, "How many of my father's hired men have food to spare, and here I am starving to death! I will set out and go back to my father and say to him: Father, I have sinned against heaven and against you. I am no longer worthy to be called your son; make me like one of your hired men." So he got up and went to his father. But while he was still a long way off, his father saw him and was*

filled with compassion for him; he ran to his son, threw his arms around him and kissed him. The son said to him, "Father, I have sinned against heaven and against you. I am no longer worthy to be called your son." But the father said to his servants, "Quick! Bring the best robe and put it on him. Put a ring on his finger and sandals on his feet. Bring the fattened calf and kill it. Let's have a feast and celebrate. For this son of mine was dead and is alive again; he was lost and is found." So they began to celebrate (Luke 15:17-24).

1. In the story of the prodigal son, the son took his inheritance and squandered the wealth on the ways of this world. After he squandered the money, he had to eat with the pigs. According to these verses, how did he feel about his relationship with his father?

2. What was he going to ask his father to make him?

3. What was the response of the father when he saw his son?

4. Did the father feel that the son was no longer worthy to be called his son?

5. How did the father celebrate the return of his son?

6. Do you think our Heavenly Father has the same attitude toward us as the father did for the prodigal son?

7. Even though we sin and go off and do our own things, from God's vantage point does this make us a slave again, or are we still His sons?

8. When we sin, do we sometimes feel exactly like the prodigal son did—that we are no longer worthy to be called God's sons?

9. God redeemed us so we would have the full rights of being a son. Therefore, how important is it for us to understand that we have been redeemed?

> *What then? Shall we sin because we are not under law but under grace? By no means! Don't you know that when you offer yourselves to someone to obey him as slaves, you are slaves to the one whom you obey—whether you are slaves to sin, which leads to death, or to obedience, which leads to righteousness? But thanks be to God that, though you used to be slaves to sin, you wholeheartedly obeyed the form of teaching to which you were entrusted. You have been set free from sin and have become slaves to righteousness* (Romans 6:15-18).

1. The constant criticism concerning the teaching of grace and our identity in Christ is that it gives a license to sin. What was Paul's response to those who asked the question, "Shall we sin because we are not under law but under grace?"

2. Paul explained his emphatic answer using the idea of slavery. How can we become a slave to a person?

3. What two options does Paul give as to whose slave we can become?

4. What did we used to be slaves to?

5. By obeying the gospel, what have we become slaves to?

6. What were we set free from?

7. This is what redemption is all about. Christ redeemed us and set us free from the law of sin and death. Does it make sense to go back to what we once were slaves to? In other words, once you have been set free from sin and death, why would you want to go back to a lifestyle of sin?

8. How does knowing you are redeemed help you to decide not to sin when you are tempted?

> *Flee from sexual immorality. All other sins a man commits are outside his body, but he who sins sexually sins against his own body. Do you not know that your body is a temple of the Holy Spirit, who is in you, whom you have received from God? You are not your own; you were bought at a price. Therefore honor God with your body* (1 Corinthians 6:18-20).

1. Paul admonishes us as children of God to flee from sexual immorality. How does he explain sexual sins in contrast to all other sins?

2. How does Paul describe your body if you are a child of God?

3. Because God has given us the Holy Spirit, what does Paul conclude about who owns us?

4. Paul says you were bought with a price. What price did God pay to purchase you and me?

5. The price God paid was His Son dying on the cross. That is what it cost God to purchase us. This is our redemption. Because we have been purchased at a price, what attitude should we develop about the actions we take in this body of flesh?

6. In light of the fact we have been redeemed and bought with a price, does it make sense to honor God with your body?

7. How does knowing you have been redeemed affect your decisions concerning sexual sins and all other sins?

8. Does knowing you are redeemed give you a license to sin, or does knowing you are redeemed develop a heart attitude that says, "I want to honor God with my body"?

> *Because you are sons, God sent the Spirit of his Son into our hearts, the Spirit who calls out, "Abba, Father." So you are no longer a slave, but a son; and since you are a son, God has made you also an heir* (Galatians 4:6,7).

1. God redeemed us that we might receive the full rights of sons. What did God do to assure us we are truly His sons?

2. Because we are sons, can we ever be slaves again?

3. Therefore, will God ever treat us as a slave?

4. And since you are a son, what has God also made you?

5. In your own words, state how knowing you are redeemed affects your relationship with God and your day-to-day living in this world.

Knowing we have been bought by the precious blood of Jesus and we are free from the law of sin and death enables us to enjoy the riches of God's love and grace. In light of the fact we have been redeemed, it just doesn't make sense to go back to what we were once enslaved to.

8

You Are Sanctified

To be sanctified means to be set apart or to be made holy. As a child of God, you have been made holy by the blood of Jesus. Holiness is not something we can attain by our own good works. Holiness is a free gift, just like salvation, that is given to all who put their faith in Christ Jesus. Knowing we have been sanctified once and for all frees us from constantly having to keep our eyes on the way we are behaving. It causes us to look to Christ and what He is doing in and through us. Let's take a closer look at some Scriptures that speak about our holy standing before God.

Key Verse: Colossians 1:22

But now he has reconciled you by Christ's physical body through death to present you holy in his sight, without blemish and free from accusation.

1. What did Christ's physical death accomplish?

2. How does God see us?

3. Is there anything that God can accuse us of?

4. How should this affect the way we see ourselves?

> *. . . who has saved us and called us to a holy life—not because of anything we have done but because of his own purpose and grace. This grace was given us in Christ Jesus before the beginning of time* (2 Timothy 1:9).

1. What kind of life has God called us to?

2. Is this something we can accomplish on our own?

3. For what reason did God save us and make us holy?

4. Who was this grace given through?

5. When was it given?

6. In light of this verse, does it make much sense to boast about our own good works?

> *And by that will, we have been made holy through the sacrifice of the body of Jesus Christ once for all* (Hebrews 10:10).

1. How were we made holy?

2. How many times were we made holy?

3. For how long?

4. Is there anything you can do to become unholy?

> *Both the one who makes men holy and those who are made holy are of the same family. So Jesus is not ashamed to call them brothers* (Hebrews 2:11).

1. What family is referred to in this verse?

2. How can Jesus be called our brother?

3. If we are part of the same family and Jesus is our brother, how should this affect our relationships with other believers?

> *To the church of God in Corinth, to those sanctified in Christ Jesus and called to be holy, together with all those everywhere who call on the name of our Lord Jesus Christ—their Lord and ours* (1 Corinthians 1:2).

The Corinthian church had many problems. Paul wrote 1 and 2 Corinthians to address these problems. One of the major concerns of Paul was the sexual immorality that was being tolerated.

1. Aware of the situation in Corinth, what does Paul say their position is in Christ Jesus?

2. What were they called to be?

3. What do all those who call on the name of the Lord Jesus Christ have in common?

4. How should knowing you are already holy affect your actions?

> *Husbands, love your wives, just as Christ loved the church and gave himself up for her to make her holy, cleansing her by the washing with water through the word, and to present her to himself as a radiant church, without stain or wrinkle or any other blemish, but holy and blameless* (Ephesians 5:25-27).

1. What did Christ do as an act of love?

2. What was the result of this action?

3. What are some adjectives used in this passage to describe the church?

4. Can these be used to describe each individual member?

5. If this is how God sees us, would it be presumptuous to see ourselves in the same way?

> *Do you not know that the wicked will not inherit the kingdom of God? Do not be deceived: Neither the sexually immoral nor idolaters nor adulterers nor male prostitutes nor homosexual offenders nor thieves nor the greedy nor drunkards nor slanderers nor swindlers will*

inherit the kingdom of God. And that is what some of you were. But you were washed, you were sanctified, you were justified in the name of the Lord Jesus Christ and by the Spirit of our God (1 Corinthians 6:9-11).

1. According to these verses, who will not inherit the kingdom of God?

2. Many of those in the church of Corinth would have been included in this list. How did their identity change?

3. How does our identity change?

4. As children of God, is our identity based on behavior?

5. Have you noticed that when you sin, instead of saying, "I stole something," Satan tries to change our identity to a thief? If you are a thief what does this passage say will happen to you?

6. Regardless of whether you have stolen something, what is your identity if you are in Christ?

He who has been stealing must steal no longer, but must work, doing something useful with his own hands, that he may have something to share with those in need (Ephesians 4:28).

1. What is God's response to a child of God who has stolen?

2. Does He call such a person a thief?

3. What does He say to do if you have been stealing?

4. How does knowing you are a child of God affect your response to God when you sin?

Rather than a standard to live up to, the holiness of God is a gift that has been given to all who believe on the Lord Jesus Christ. As we have seen, we are sanctified by our faith in Him, not by our good works. Therefore, our identity is based on what He has done rather than on what we do.

9

You Are Justified

To be justified means to be made right with God. Our identity before coming to Christ was that of a sinner. As it says in Ephesians 2:3, "We were by nature objects of wrath." Having been born in sin, we were cut off from the life of God. However, through the death, burial, and resurrection of Jesus Christ, we have been brought back into a right relationship with God. Because Jesus took all of our sin and gave us His righteousness, we stand before God justified.

Key Verse: Romans 5:18

Consequently, just as the result of one trespass was condemnation for all men, so also the result of one act of righteousness was justification that brings life for all men.

1. What was the result of one man's sin?

2. How many people did it affect?

3. What was the result of one act of righteousness?

4. How many people did it affect?

5. Who performed this one act?

6. What does justification bring?

> ... *so that, having been justified by his grace, we might become heirs having the hope of eternal life* (Titus 3:7).

1. What are we justified by?

2. Once we are justified, what do we become?

3. What does it mean to be an heir?

4. What is our hope?

Justification is a free gift. It is not based on anything we do or even our observance of the law. It can only be received by faith in what Christ did on our behalf.

> *Know that a man is not justified by observing the law, but by faith in Jesus Christ. So we, too, have put our faith in Christ Jesus that we may*

> *be justified by faith in Christ and not by observing the law, because by observing the law no one will be justified* (Galatians 2:16).

1. Can a man be justified by observing the law?

2. How is a man justified?

3. Why can't we be justified by observing the law?

> *You who are trying to be justified by law have been alienated from Christ; you have fallen away from grace* (Galatians 5:4).

1. According to this verse, when someone seeks to be justified by the law, what have they done?

2. Can you try to be justified by law and rest in the fact that you have been justified by faith in Christ at the same time?

3. Those who try to be justified by law have fallen away from what?

4. What does this verse say to someone who is trying to mix law and grace?

5. Does "fallen away" mean loss of salvation, or does it mean a person has turned away from the truth?

6. In light of these last two verses, does the law play any role in our justification?

Therefore, since we have been justified through faith, we have peace with God through our Lord Jesus Christ (Romans 5:1).

1. Who do we have peace with now that we are justified?

2. If you have peace with God, how should this affect your relationship with Him?

3. Is there any reason to be afraid of God now that you have peace with Him?

What, then, shall we say in response to this? If God is for us, who can be against us? He who did not spare his own Son, but gave him up for us all—how will he not also, along with him, graciously give us all things? Who will bring any charge against those whom God has chosen? It is God who justifies. Who is he that condemns? Christ Jesus, who died—more than that, who was raised to life—is at the right hand of God and is also interceding for us (Romans 8:31-34).

1. Since you have been justified, can you conclude that God is for you?

2. If God is for you, does it matter if anyone is against you?

3. Can anyone accuse you?

4. If God has declared us totally righteous, does it matter what Satan or anybody else says?

> *For all have sinned and fall short of the glory of God, and are justified freely by his grace through the redemption that came by Christ Jesus* (Romans 3:23,24).

1. How many people have sinned and fallen short of the glory of God?

2. How are these same people justified?

3. Who offers this redemption?

4. If all of us, born sinners, are justified in the same way, how should this affect the way we look at others?

As we have seen, understanding we are justified not only affects our relationship with God but also our relationships with others. Knowing you are in right standing before God, not because of what you have done but because of Christ's work on the cross, is what frees you to enjoy that perfect fellowship with Him. It is much easier to be at peace with man when you know you are at peace with God.

10

You Are Part
of the Body of Christ

There is a desire in the heart of every human to be a part of something, to fit into some group. That sense of belonging motivates people to join country clubs, civic clubs, college fraternities and sororities, gangs, and even churches. As part of our inheritance and identity in Christ, God meets our need to belong.

Through your faith in Jesus Christ, you have been placed into the body of Christ. The body of Christ is not an organization, but a living organism made up of people all around the world and throughout history who have named the name of Christ. You will be part of the body of Christ throughout eternity.

Key Verse: 1 Corinthians 12:27

Now you are the body of Christ, and each one of you is a part of it.

1. According to this verse, who is the body of Christ?

2. Who makes up the parts of the body of Christ?

3. What can we conclude about our relationships to one another since each one of us is a part of the body of Christ?

> *The body is a unit, though it is made up of many parts; and though all its parts are many, they form one body. So it is with Christ. For we were all baptized by one Spirit into one body—whether Jews or Greeks, slave or free—and we were all given the one Spirit to drink* (1 Corinthians 12:12,13).

1. How does Paul describe the body?

2. What is our physical body made up of?

3. Even though there are many parts, these parts come together to form what?

4. What does Paul compare our physical bodies to?

5. How did you and I become a part of the body of Christ?

6. Regardless of our backgrounds—whether Jews, Greeks, slave or free—what unifies us?

Each of us comes to Christ on an individual basis. Regardless of background, every person who places his faith in Jesus Christ is indwelt by the Spirit of God. Romans 8:9 says that if anyone does not have the Spirit of God, he does not belong to Christ. You cannot be a Christian apart from God's Spirit living in you.

Once the Spirit of God comes to live inside a person, the Spirit of God in turn places that person into the body of Christ. We come to Christ on an individual basis, but then we are joined to the body of Christ. As a result, we can say we belong to Christ, and we belong to one another.

> *Is not the cup of thanksgiving for which we give thanks a participation in the blood of Christ? And is not the bread that we break a participation in the body of Christ? Because there is one loaf, we, who are many, are one body, for we all partake of the one loaf* (1 Corinthians 10:16,17).

1. In the Lord's Supper, what does the cup of thanksgiving represent?

2. What does the bread represent?

3. Because we have all partaken of the one loaf, what do we, who are many, become?

4. How does participating in the Lord's Supper show us the truth that we belong to Christ, and we belong to one another?

> *And he is the head of the body, the church; he is the beginning and the firstborn from among the dead, so that in everything he might have the supremacy* (Colossians 1:18).

1. According to this verse, who is the head of the body?

2. Who has the supremacy in everything?

3. Therefore, who directs all the parts of the body?

> *Just as each of us has one body with many members, and these members do not all have the same function, so in Christ we who are many form one body, and each member belongs to all the others. We*

have different gifts, according to the grace given us. If a man's gift is prophesying, let him use it in proportion to his faith. If it is serving, let him serve; if it is teaching, let him teach; if it is encouraging, let him encourage; if it is contributing to the needs of others, let him give generously; if it is leadership, let him govern diligently; if it is showing mercy, let him do it cheerfully (Romans 12:4-8).

1. As in the book of Corinthians, Paul here compares the body of Christ to our physical bodies. Do the different parts of our body all have the same function?

2. In Christ, because we form one body, what is our relationship to one another?

3. Even though we form one body, do we all have the same function or gift?

4. What gifts does Paul list in these verses?

5. What should our attitude be toward someone who has the gift of serving, for example?

6. Since Christ is the head of the body, if someone has the gift of serving (or teaching or any other gift listed in these verses), who can we conclude is directing that person to serve?

7. How does knowing that you are a part of the body of Christ, and that Christ directs each part as He sees fit, affect your attitude toward others?

Let the peace of Christ rule in your hearts, since as members of one body you were called to peace. And be thankful (Colossians 3:15).

1. What does Paul say we are to let rule in our hearts?

2. What is the foundation for allowing the peace of Christ to rule in our hearts?

3. As members of one body, what were we called to?

4. What is the resulting attitude towards one another when we recognize that we are members of one body?

> *Therefore each of you must put off falsehood and speak truthfully to his neighbor, for we are all members of one body* (Ephesians 4:25).

1. What does this verse tell us to do?

2. How should we speak to one another?

3. What is the reason we should speak truthfully?

> *From him the whole body, joined and held together by every supporting ligament, grows and builds itself up in love, as each part does its work* (Ephesians 4:16).

1. What is the result when each part does its work?

2. When each part does its work, what does the body build itself up in?

3. Where does the growth and the building up in love come from?

4. Based on the verses we have studied in this chapter, how important is it to know that part of your identity in Christ is that you are part of the body of Christ?

11

You Are a Citizen of Heaven

___

Once we have been placed into Christ, our citizenship is no longer in this world. We have a new home that awaits us in heaven. This should give us a new perspective on how we deal with day-to-day life. It is easy to get caught up in our daily struggles and forget that all of it is just temporary. The Word of God has much to say about heaven and who it is prepared for.

___

Key Verse: Philippians 3:20

But our citizenship is in heaven. And we eagerly await a Savior from there, the Lord Jesus Christ.

___

1. As children of God, where is our citizenship?

2. What are we awaiting?

3. How does knowing our citizenship is in heaven and we are waiting for Christ to return to take us there affect our attitude toward the things of this world?

> *Praise be to the God and Father of our Lord Jesus Christ! In his great mercy he has given us new birth into a living hope through the resurrection of Jesus Christ from the dead, and into an inheritance that can never perish, spoil or fade—kept in heaven for you* (1 Peter 1:3,4).

1. How does Peter describe our inheritance in Christ Jesus?

2. Where is this inheritance kept?

3. How does someone gain this inheritance?

4. How does this inheritance differ from all earthly treasures?

> *But you have come to Mount Zion, to the heavenly Jerusalem, the city of the living God. You have come to thousands upon thousands of angels in joyful assembly, to the church of the firstborn, whose names are written in heaven. You have come to God, the judge of all men, to the spirits of righteous men made perfect* (Hebrews 12:22,23).

Mount Zion is used in this passage to contrast the old and the new covenant. The old covenant was given to Moses at Mount Sinai and represents the law; Mount Zion is representative of the new covenant and the heavenly city of God and those who dwell there with Him.

1. How is the church described in this passage?

2. Where are our names written?

3. If our names are already written in heaven, how should this affect our understanding of who we are in Christ?

> *That day will bring about the destruction of the heavens by fire, and the elements will melt in the heat. But in keeping with his promise we are looking forward to a new heaven and a new earth, the home of righteousness* (2 Peter 3:12,13).

1. What will happen one day to the heavens and the earth?

2. Is this something that will affect us as children of God?

3. Why not?

4. What should we be looking forward to?

5. Whose home is the new heaven and the new earth?

> *I consider that our present sufferings are not worth comparing with the glory that will be revealed in us. The creation waits in eager expectation for the sons of God to be revealed. For the creation was subjected to frustration, not by its own choice, but by the will of the one who subjected it, in hope that the creation itself will be liberated from its bondage to decay and brought into the glorious freedom of the children of God. We know that the whole creation has been groaning as in the pains of childbirth right up to the present time. Not only so, but we ourselves, who have the firstfruits of the Spirit, groan inwardly as we wait eagerly for our adoption as sons, the redemption of our bodies* (Romans 8:18-23).

1. How did Paul view his present sufferings and tribulations?

2. How could he view life in this way?

3. How should we view our present trials and tribulations?

4. What is our hope as children of God for ourselves and for creation?

5. Although the environment and the political situations are getting worse by the day, should this be something that should overly concern us?

Because we are citizens of heaven, we need not get too involved in the things of this world. It is God's job to change the world, which He will ultimately do. Our mission is to proclaim the good news of the Kingdom of God, which is the only thing that can bring lasting change to men's hearts.

> *Now we know that if the earthly tent we live in is destroyed, we have a building from God, an eternal house in heaven, not built by human hands* (2 Corinthians 5:1).

1. What does Paul mean by "the earthly tent"?

2. How is it destroyed?

3. How is the earthly tent different from the eternal house?

4. Who is the eternal house in heaven built for?

5. If God has prepared a home in heaven for all those who put their faith in Christ, what does this tell us about Him?

Knowing that our names are written in heaven and that we have a guaranteed home when we leave this earth is a great comfort. More than just a comfort, it gives us the freedom to walk in confidence that this earth is not our home. We can live above our circumstances because we have an eternal perspective. Our identity is not based on circumstances but on the unchanging promises of God.

12

You Have Eternal Life

A question that haunts the minds of many people is, "How do I know for sure that I have eternal life?" It is a question that keeps many people in bondage to the fear of death. However, the Bible is very clear when it comes to this issue. God never intended us to doubt the quality of life Jesus Christ gives us. In order for our identity to be secure in Christ, we must come to an understanding of what eternal life really means. God answers these questions through His Word and His Spirit.

Key Verse: 1 John 5:11-13

And this is the testimony: God has given us eternal life, and this life is in his Son. He who has the Son has life; he who does not have the Son of God does not have life. I write these things to you who believe in the name of the Son of God so that you may know that you have eternal life.

1. What is God's testimony concerning eternal life?

2. What do you have if you have the Son?

3. If you do not have the Son, what do you not have?

4. Why did John write these things?

> *For God so loved the world that he gave his one and only Son, that whoever believes in him shall not perish but have eternal life* (John 3:16).

1. What was the motivation for God sending His only Son to die for our sins?

2. Who is this verse speaking to?

3. What is it that saves us from perishing?

4. What do we have when we believe on Christ?

Eternal life is just that—it is *eternal*. If eternal life could be lost, it would have to be temporal life. We can be secure that the eternal life we have been given in Christ can never be taken away from us.

> *I give them eternal life, and they shall never perish; no one can snatch them out of my hand* (John 10:28).

1. Who has the power to give eternal life?

2. Once we have eternal life, can we ever perish?

3. Can anyone or anything cause you to lose eternal life?

4. Does that "anyone" include yourself?

For the wages of sin is death, but the gift of God is eternal life in Christ Jesus our Lord (Romans 6:23).

1. What are the wages of sin?

2. What is the gift of God?

3. Where is eternal life found?

4. Therefore, if you have received Christ Jesus, what did you receive?

Wages are earned, but a gift is given freely. In his best efforts, man can only earn death and destruction. Eternal life cannot be earned; it can only be given freely by God to those who would accept it.

In the same way, count yourselves dead to sin but alive to God in Christ Jesus (Romans 6:11).

1. The reason we can know we have eternal life is because the thing that killed us (sin) has been dealt with once and for all. If sin had not been forgiven and taken away, what would happen each time we sinned?

2. How can we know we have eternal life even when we sin?

The thief comes only to steal and kill and destroy; I have come that they may have life, and have it to the full (John 10:10).

1. What is it that Satan comes to do?

2. What did Jesus come to do?

3. What, then, should we be preoccupied with, sin (that He came to take away) or life (that He came to give us)?

> *So that, just as sin reigned in death, so also grace might reign through righteousness to bring eternal life through Jesus Christ our Lord* (Romans 5:21).

1. Since sin's reign leads to death, and we were all born in sin, what is our natural state?

2. What does the grace of God bring?

3. If our natural state is death because of sin, what do we have if we have been placed into Christ?

4. What does this tell us about man's ability to gain eternal life on his own?

> *For my Father's will is that everyone who looks to the Son and believes in him shall have eternal life, and I will raise him up at the last day* (John 6:40).

1. What is the Father's will?

2. What will God do at the last day if we have put our faith in Christ?

3. How should this affect our attitude toward death?

4. How should this affect our relationship with God?

   As we have seen, eternal life is found only in Christ. Therefore, since Christ lives in us, we have eternal life. The two cannot be separated. Eternal life begins the moment we accept Christ into our hearts by faith. Understanding this reality will free us from the fear of death and give us an eternal perspective on life.

13

You Are
Totally Loved

Our identity in Christ is based on the love of God. Everything we have learned thus far about who we are in Christ is the result of God's love. It was love that motivated God to make us His children and to give us this incredible inheritance. Anytime we have doubts concerning our identity—whether it is questioning our forgiveness, wondering about our righteous standing before God, or fearing we have lost our salvation—what we are really questioning is God's love for us: "Does He totally love me and accept me in this situation or doesn't He?" We have all asked this question at times. So you can see why it is so important to realize that part of our identity as believers is that we are totally loved by God.

Key Verse: John 15:9

As the Father has loved me, so have I loved you. Now remain in my love.

1. What did Jesus equate His love for us to?

2. How much love do you think God the Father has for His Son Jesus Christ?

3. Based on the previous question, how much love do you think Jesus Christ has for you?

4. Because of the great love Jesus has for us, what does He encourage us to do?

5. Why do you think Jesus told us to remain in His love for us?

6. In your own life, have there been times you have questioned God's love for you?

7. During those times, did God's love for you ever change or stop?

8. Therefore, how important is it to remain in God's love?

> *And I pray that you, being rooted and established in love, may have power, together with all the saints, to grasp how wide and long and high and deep is the love of Christ, and to know this love that surpasses knowledge—that you may be filled to the measure of all the fullness of God* (Ephesians 3:17-19).

1. As children of God, what are we to be rooted and established in?

2. What did Paul pray that we might have?

3. According to these verses, why do we need power?

4. Could you understand how wide and long and high and deep the love of Christ is for you apart from the power of God to do so?

5. Not only does Paul pray we will grasp what the love of God is, but he also prays this love will do what?

6. In your own life, when does the love of God surpass knowledge?

7. To know the love of God that surpasses knowledge means that God's love has become a part of your day-to-day experience. What is the result of knowing and experiencing the love of God?

Christ tells us to remain in His love. However, we cannot understand how high and wide and deep and long Christ's love for us truly is through our finite minds. As 1 Corinthians 2:9,10 states, " 'No eye has seen, no ear has heard, no mind has conceived what God has prepared for those who love Him'—but God has revealed it to us by his Spirit." God has given us the power to understand and experience His love for us through His Holy Spirit. But what is the love of God? Let's take a look at the definition of love in the Bible and see exactly how God loves us.

> *Love is patient, love is kind. It does not envy, it does not boast, it is not proud. It is not rude, it is not self-seeking, it is not easily angered, it keeps no record of wrongs. Love does not delight in evil but rejoices with the truth. It always protects, always trusts, always hopes, always perseveres* (1 Corinthians 13:4-7).

1. The most common application of these verses is how we should love others. First and foremost, however, 1 Corinthians 13 describes how God loves us. According to these verses, how does God love you?

2. The Bible tells us that God is love. To help you gain a deeper understanding of God's love, reread these verses, substituting *God* for the word *love*. Now, write down each characteristic of God's love placing the words "with me" at the end.

God is patient with me.

3. Have you come to realize that the definition of *love* in 1 Corinthians 13 is how God loves you? If not, are you willing to do so right now?

4. Will knowing that God's love keeps no records of wrongs affect how you respond to God when you sin?

5. Does God's love—the fact that He is patient with you—assure you that He will never give up on you, even though you continue to sin every day?

6. Can you see why Jesus told us to remain in His love?

7. Will this love that God has for you ever change?

8. Do you think it is possible to pass on 1 Corinthians love to others without first receiving this love from God?

Who shall separate us from the love of Christ? Shall trouble or hardship or persecution or famine or nakedness or danger or sword? As it is written: "For your sake we face death all day long; we are considered as sheep to be slaughtered." No, in all these things we are more than conquerors through him who loved us. For I am convinced that neither death nor life, neither angels nor demons, neither the present nor the future, nor any powers, neither height nor depth, nor anything else in all creation, will be able to separate us from the love of God that is in Christ Jesus our Lord (Romans 8:35-39).

1. What question did Paul ask concerning the love of Christ?

2. Paul suffered trouble, hardship, persecution, famine, nakedness, danger, and the sword. Did any of these separate Paul from the love of God?

3. Through Him who loved him, what did Paul become in all these things?

4. In your life, has there ever been anything (for example, a particular sin or a difficult circumstance) that you thought separated you from the love of Christ?

5. If so, during those times did you feel like a conqueror or did you experience defeat in your life?

6. Through all of his experiences, what did Paul become convinced of?

7. What did Paul include in his list of things that could not separate him from the love of God?

8. Did Paul leave out anything we could encounter or experience in this life?

9. Based on Paul's list, is there anything that could separate you from the love of God?

10. Have you become convinced in your own heart that nothing can separate you from the love of God?

> *For Christ's love compels us, because we are convinced that one died for all, and therefore all died* (2 Corinthians 5:14).

1. What did Paul say compelled him?

2. What is to compel us in our daily lives?

3. It is easy to get discouraged in this world because of all the trials and tribulations, even to the point of wanting to give up. What is it that gets us through these trials and enables us, as Paul wrote in Romans 8, to become conquerors?

4. Even in the worst of circumstances, can you count on the love of God—that He is patient with you, that He is kind, that He will never keep records of your wrongs, etc.?

5. When times are bad, or even when times are good, what is the only constant you can depend on?

6. Through this study, can you see why it is so important to realize that part of your identity in Christ is that you are totally loved?

> *We love because he first loved us* (1 John 4:19).

1. What enables us to love God and others?

2. Could we love God without first receiving His love for us?

3. Could we pass on God's love to others without first resting in God's love for us?

4. According to this verse, if you are having problems loving God or others, what is the root reason?

If you love me, you will obey what I command (John 14:15).

1. According to this verse, what is the result of loving God?

2. What is more important—obeying what God commands or learning to love Christ?

A love for God is produced in our hearts when we respond to God's love for us. It is impossible to love God without an understanding of God's love for us. As we respond to God's love, it becomes easy to obey Christ's command, which is to love one another.

My command is this: Love each other as I have loved you (John 15:12).

1. What is Christ's command to us?

2. How are we to love one another?

3. In learning to love others, what must our focus be?

How great is the love the Father has lavished on us, that we should be called children of God! And that is what we are! (1 John 3:1).

1. How does the Father lavish His love on us?

2. How does John describe this love that calls us children of God?

3. Why do you think John was so emphatic in his declaration of our identity?

4. If you are a child of God, what can you say concerning the love of God?

5. Why is it so important to understand that your identity is a child of God?

We have an incredible identity in Christ. To be a child of God is an identity given to us by His grace and it is more wonderful than we could ever imagine. Knowing who you are in Christ enables you to know that you are totally loved and accepted by God. Don't settle for anything less! And don't allow Satan or the world to tell you that you are something other than a child of God. It is an identity based on His absolute truth, and you can rest assured that it will never change.

—*Also from Bob George*—
Discover the
Good News of the Grace of God!

CLASSIC CHRISTIANITY

Why do so many Christians start out as enthusiastic believers and end up merely "going through the motions"? In his down-to-earth style, Bob George shows us the way back to authentic Christianity—the kind that Christ had in mind when He set us free.

GROWING IN GRACE

Picking up where *Classic Christianity* left off, *Growing in Grace* helps Christians *live out* their freedom in Christ in the face of daily pressures and circumstances of life. Bob George offers a picture of daily Christian life that is completely within your grasp.